BALD EAGLE VS. STELLER'S SEA EAGLE

BY NATHAN SOMMER

BELLWETHER MEDIA • MINNEAPOLIS, MN

Torque brims with excitement
perfect for thrill-seekers of all kinds.
Discover daring survival skills, explore
uncharted worlds, and marvel at mighty
engines and extreme sports. In *Torque* books,
anything can happen. Are you ready?

This edition first published in 2025 by Bellwether Media, Inc.

Library of Congress Cataloging-in-Publication Data

LC record for Bald Eagle vs. Steller's Sea Eagle available at:
https://lccn.loc.gov/2024019783

Editor: Suzane Nguyen   Designer: Hunter Demmin

Printed in the United States of America, North Mankato, MN.

TABLE OF CONTENTS

THE COMPETITORS

Eagles are **fierce** birds. Bald eagles **soar** high and fly at top speeds to easily catch most **prey**. They use size and speed to hunt.

Bald eagles sometimes share the skies with Steller's sea eagles. Steller's sea eagles use size and strength to overpower other birds. Which eagle is tougher?

Bald eagles are large **raptors**. They have white heads and long, hooked beaks. Their sturdy bodies have broad wings. Their wingspans reach up to 8 feet (2.4 meters) wide.

Bald eagles are found throughout North America. The birds build nests high up in trees or on cliffs near water.

NEST FOR LIFE

Bald eagles often use the same nests for their entire lives. Some nests weigh up to 4,000 pounds (1,814 kilograms)!

BALD EAGLE PROFILE

|---|---|---|---|---|
| 0 | 2 FEET | 4 FEET | 6 FEET | 8 FEET |

WINGSPAN
UP TO 8 FEET
(2.4 METERS)

WEIGHT
UP TO 14 POUNDS
(6.4 KILOGRAMS)

HEIGHT
AROUND 3 FEET
(0.9 METERS)

HABITATS

COASTS   WETLANDS   FORESTS   GRASSLANDS

BALD EAGLE RANGE

STELLER'S SEA EAGLE PROFILE

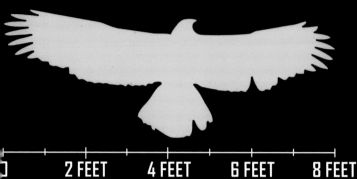

2 FEET	4 FEET	6 FEET	8 FEET

WINGSPAN
UP TO 8 FEET
(2.4 METERS)

WEIGHT
UP TO 20 POUNDS
(9.1 KILOGRAMS)

HEIGHT
AROUND 3.1 FEET
(1 METER)

HABITATS

COASTS

WETLANDS

ROCKY AREAS

STELLER'S SEA EAGLE RANGE

RANGE

8

Steller's sea eagles are the world's heaviest eagles. These powerful birds weigh up to 20 pounds (9.1 kilograms). They have dark brown bodies. Their tails, legs, and shoulders are white. Their eyes and large beaks are golden.

Steller's sea eagles mostly live in parts of Japan, Korea, and Russia. They prefer **habitats** near rivers and coastlines.

RARE EAGLES

There are less than 5,000 Steller's sea eagles left in the wild.

SECRET WEAPONS

EAGLE VS. HUMAN VISION

Bald eagles can see four times farther than humans.

Bald eagles use excellent vision to find prey. They can spot fish from 1 mile (1.6 kilometers) away! Three eyelids keep their eyes safe from strong winds and dust.

Steller's sea eagles use strong wings to travel long distances. These birds **migrate** every winter. They may fly from Russia to Japan!

Broad wings help bald eagles soar easily and save **energy** while hunting. The wings also help them dive quickly. The birds can reach speeds of up to 100 miles (161 kilometers) per hour!

BALD EAGLE WINGSPAN VS. HUMAN HEIGHT

8 FEET
(2.4 METERS)

6 FEET
(1.8 METERS)

STELLER'S SEA EAGLE BEAK SIZE

4.5 INCHES
(11.4 CENTIMETERS)

Steller's sea eagles have some of the largest beaks of all eagles. Their beaks grow up to 4.5 inches (11.4 centimeters) long. The birds use these to cut through prey.

VISION

BROAD WINGS

SHARP TALONS

Bald eagles have sharp **talons**. They squeeze their talons tightly around prey. The birds can carry prey weighing up to 4 pounds (1.8 kilograms).

SECRET WEAPONS

STRONG WINGS

LARGE BEAKS

SPICULES

Steller's sea eagles have **spicules**. These special foot bumps help them hold slippery fish without dropping them. The birds can fly at high speeds without losing prey.

ATTACK MOVES

Bald eagles are **opportunistic** hunters. They hunt whatever they can catch. The birds **perch** in trees or on cliffs. Then, they quickly swoop down once they spot prey!

Steller's sea eagles are one of the most **aggressive** eagles. They use their size to attack other birds. They are known to steal food from other animals!

Bald eagles snatch fish from water with their open talons. They close their talons around prey until it is defeated. The birds then use their beaks to slice through captured prey.

DEAD OR ALIVE

Bald eagles and Steller's sea eagles eat dead animals when food is hard to find.

Steller's sea eagles mostly eat fish. They often stand in shallow water. Then, they grab fish swimming by with their beaks!

A Steller's sea eagle spots a bald eagle flying with prey. The sea eagle quickly dives down. It is going to try to steal a meal.

The sea eagle bites the bald eagle. The bald eagle fights back! It scratches the sea eagle with a sharp talon. The hurt sea eagle flies away. No one steals this bald eagle's prey!

GLOSSARY

aggressive—ready to fight

energy—the power needed to do something

fierce—strong and intense

habitats—the homes or areas where animals prefer to live

migrate—to travel from one place to another, often with the seasons

opportunistic—taking advantage of a situation

perch—to sit in a high place

prey—animals that are hunted by other animals for food

raptors—large birds that hunt other animals; raptors are also called birds of prey.

soar—to fly without flapping wings

spicules—tiny spines on the bottom of some birds' feet; spicules help birds carry slippery prey.

talons—sharp claws on birds that allow them to grab and tear into prey

TO LEARN MORE

AT THE LIBRARY

Clasky, Leonard. *Bald Eagle*. New York, N.Y.: Gareth Stevens Publishing, 2023.

Lukidis, Lydia. *Eagles*. Mankato, Minn.: Black Rabbit Books, 2023.

Sommer, Nathan. *Golden Eagle vs. Great Horned Owl*. Minneapolis, Minn.: Bellwether Media, 2021.

ON THE WEB

FACTSURFER

Factsurfer.com gives you a safe, fun way to find more information.

1. Go to www.factsurfer.com

2. Enter "bald eagle vs. Steller's sea eagle" into the search box and click $\mathcal{Q}$.

3. Select your book cover to see a list of related web sites.

INDEX